Original title:
Rain's Solace

Copyright © 2024 Swan Charm
All rights reserved.

Author: Aron Pilviste
ISBN HARDBACK: 978-9908-1-2602-9
ISBN PAPERBACK: 978-9908-1-2603-6
ISBN EBOOK: 978-9908-1-2604-3

Inundated Goodbyes

Waves crash on the shore,
Memories linger near.
Voices lost in the roar,
Each farewell draws a tear.

Raindrops blend with the sea,
Echoes of what once was.
Parting brings hearts to plea,
Caught in a silent buzz.

Fading footprints in sand,
Time washes them away.
Holding tightly the hand,
Of moments that won't stay.

Clouds hang heavy and gray,
Sky weeps with our release.
Drifting further each day,
Inundated by peace.

In the haze, we depart,
As shadows start to blend.
An ache within the heart,
Goodbyes that never end.

Skies that Speak

Clouds whisper secrets low,
Painting the world above.
With each gentle glow,
They tell tales of lost love.

Stars wink in the deep night,
Guiding dreams with their light.
Every spark, a delight,
A promise held so tight.

The sun spills golden beams,
Amongst the waking trees.
Nature hums soft themes,
Carried on evening's breeze.

Raindrops tap on the pane,
Each one sings a refrain.
In the joy and the pain,
The skies share their disdain.

Thunder thunders a laugh,
Lightning dances bold ways.
Nature's own autograph,
In vibrant, wild displays.

Circles in the Wet Earth

Beneath the weeping sky,
Footprints form a soft trace.
With every drop on high,
Nature finds its embrace.

Waves ripple on the ground,
Creating life beneath.
In patterns they are found,
A dance of quiet breath.

Leaves sway with gentle grace,
Softly touching the mud.
A moment's sweet embrace,
In the after-rain flood.

In the twilight's stillness,
Ripples reflect a thought.
Circles tell a witness,
To what time has wrought.

From puddles, dreams arise,
Each one a fleeting spark.
In the ground, the skies,
Mark stories in the dark.

A Soft Soliloquy

Whispers float through the air,
Thoughts drift like autumn leaves.
In the silence I share,
My heart's truth quietly weaves.

Moonlight bathes the night plain,
Casting shadows so light,
Each word softly ingrained,
In the fabric of night.

A breeze speaks gentle sighs,
Carrying secrets of old.
Time hides where the heart lies,
In stories waiting to be told.

Moments slip through my hands,
Like grains of soft, fine sand.
Each echo softly stands,
In a dream's warm, whispered land.

In this quiet retreat,
I find solace alone.
A soliloquy sweet,
In the stillness, I've grown.

Timeless Trickle

A brook flows soft and low,
Whispers of stories untold.
Pebbles dance beneath the glow,
Time's secret, etched in gold.

Gentle ripples sing their song,
Carving paths through ancient stone.
Nature's pulse, steady and strong,
In simplicity, we're not alone.

Leaves flutter, kissed by the breeze,
Each drop reflects the sky's hue.
The world bends, it ceases to freeze,
As moments drift, endless and new.

Waters play, a symphony clear,
Echoes of laughter abound.
In every flow, love draws near,
A timeless trickle, profound.

Nature holds her heart wide open,
Inviting us to hear and see.
In every bend, a promise spoken,
Eternity flows, wild and free.

A Solitary Path in the Storm

Rain falls heavy, clouds churn grey,
The world trembles beneath its weight.
One figure walks, come what may,
An anchor in fate's fickle state.

Winds howl like a mournful song,
Yet determination lights the way.
Each step forward feels so strong,
Against the tempest's fierce ballet.

Puddles form, reflections dance,
A mirror of chaos and might.
With each breath, a steady chance,
To face the darkness, seek the light.

Thunder rolls, a drumming heart,
But courage stirs within the soul.
In storms, new beginnings start,
Lone traveler, embracing whole.

The path is steep, the journey long,
Yet with resolve, spirits fly.
Alone, but never truly wrong,
In the storm's embrace, we rise high.

Veins of Water on the Earth

Rivers trace the ancient ground,
Like veins pulsing, life flows near.
Through valleys deep, the waters sound,
Life's essence whispers, crystal clear.

Every droplet, a tale to tell,
Of mountain tops and winding streams.
In nature's rhythm, all is well,
The pulse of earth, woven in dreams.

When sunlight graces the surface bright,
Reflections shimmer, a dance alive.
In every turn, a spark of light,
Veins of water, where life will thrive.

From melted snow to oceans wide,
Journeying fast, or slow and still.
In every ebb, a chance to guide,
Through spirals of fate, we find our will.

From roots to leaves, the cycle spins,
Intertwined, all beings flow.
In every drop, a spark begins,
Veins of water, forever aglow.

Morning's Invitation to the Wet World

Dewdrops cling to blades of grass,
A fresh embrace held tight and clear.
Sunlight breaks, the shadows pass,
Morning whispers, 'Come, draw near.'

Birds awaken, tunes arise,
Each note a gift from realms above.
In a canvas painted by sighs,
A melody of life and love.

The air is crisp, filled with hope,
Nature opens her gentle arms.
Inviting all who dare to cope,
With wonders hiding in her charms.

In every puddle, light unfolds,
Reflections of dreams yet to bloom.
Secrets of nature's heart, it holds,
Awakening life from slumber's gloom.

Morning calls, the world anew,
Hands reach out to feel the change.
In every heart, the call rings true,
Together, we gather, feel the strange.

Shelter from the Barrel of Clouds

Beneath gray skies, the raindrops play,
Whispering secrets, soft ballet.
A refuge found, where shadows blend,
In arms of storms, we shall transcend.

Cloaked in rhythms, hearts entwined,
With every beat, the world aligned.
A dance of hope on puddled ground,
In shelter there, our peace is found.

Nature's tears, they cleanse the air,
With every sigh, a silent prayer.
Together, brave, through tempests roar,
We seek the light, forevermore.

Winds may howl, but love remains,
A bond unbroken, through the chains.
In heavy clouds, we find our way,
Through stormy nights, to brighter days.

So let the thunder echo loud,
We are the heart beneath the cloud.
With every storm, our spirits rise,
In shelter, dreams touch open skies.

Soaked Memories of Yesteryears

Raindrops tap on the windowpane,
Each one a story, joy or pain.
Against the glass, reflections show,
The past unfolds, like whispers low.

In puddles deep, we see the waves,
Of laughter lost, in sunny days.
Soaked in thoughts, we reminisce,
The warmth of moments, we can't dismiss.

Faded pictures, colors run,
Caught in storms, but still we run.
Beyond the showers, memories gleam,
In soaked embraces, love's a dream.

As clouds drift by, we search for signs,
In every droplet, our heart aligns.
Through rain-soaked paths, we walk again,
Reliving echoes, free from pain.

So let the rain cleanse all that's drear,
Each falling drop, a whispered cheer.
For in the storm, we find our way,
Through soaked memories, come what may.

The Quiet Revolution of Nature

In stillness grows a world anew,
With gentle whispers, life breaks through.
The trees stand tall, roots intertwined,
In silent strength, the earth aligned.

A cycle blooms, in colors bright,
Each petal kissed by morning light.
The softest breeze, a hidden call,
In nature's grace, we find it all.

Yet in the quiet, truths emerge,
With every heartbeat, flows a surge.
Through rustling leaves, the stories share,
A revolution in the air.

From mountains high to oceans wide,
The harmony, we cannot hide.
In stillness, strength begins to grow,
Through nature's song, we come to know.

Let us embrace this gentle force,
For in the calm, we find the source.
The quiet revolution thrives,
In nature's breath, our spirit strives.

Conversations with the Flood

In swirling waters, tales unfold,
Whispers deep, both brave and bold.
The river speaks of time gone by,
Carrying dreams beneath the sky.

With every surge, a story flows,
Of hopes and fears the current knows.
In muddy banks, lives intertwine,
With nature's voice, our hearts align.

Through torrents fierce, we find our way,
In raging waves, storm clouds play.
Conversations with the depths unseen,
Bring forth the truth, pure and keen.

Yet in the stillness, echoes sigh,
As waters dance, and pass us by.
We listen close to nature's hymn,
In floods of thought, our spirits swim.

So let the rivers guide our fate,
In flowing paths, we contemplate.
With open hearts and minds so wide,
We find our place, with the tide.

In the Company of Clouds

Above me float the clouds so bright,
Changing shapes in soft daylight.
Whispers carried on a gentle breeze,
A dance of shadows among the trees.

In the morn, they wear a golden hue,
While twilight wraps them in deep blue.
They gather close when storms arise,
A shroud of gray against the skies.

Each one tells a tale from afar,
Of distant lands and wandering stars.
Softly drifting, they softly sway,
Guardians of dreams that fade away.

In their company, I find my peace,
As burdens lift and worries cease.
In quiet moments, I gently stare,
At tender forms that linger there.

Above the world, they roam and play,
Eternal dancers, come what may.
In the company of clouds, I roam,
A fleeting heart no longer alone.

Tears of the Sky

When the heavens begin to weep,
The world below stirs from its sleep.
Pitter patter on the ground,
A symphony of solace found.

Each drop a story, each splash a song,
A reminder that the weak are strong.
They cleanse the earth with gentle grace,
Washing worries from every face.

The clouds release their heavy hearts,
As joy and sorrow blend in parts.
From grey to blue, the sky transforms,
As love and loss in rain conforms.

Children dance in puddles wide,
Finding treasure where grief resides.
Laughter mingles with the storm,
In tears of joy, new hopes are born.

So let the sky shed every tear,
For every drop brings beauty near.
In the tapestry, we find our way,
Embracing life, come what may.

Embrace of the Deluge

The deluge falls with fierce intent,
A reminder of nature's strength well-spent.
Waves of water engulf the land,
In its embrace, we take a stand.

Lightning flashes, thunder roars,
An ancient rhythm that nature pours.
Yet in the chaos, I find a calm,
A grounding force, a soothing balm.

Raindrops dance on rooftops high,
Like whispers of love from the sky.
Each droplet weaves a tale anew,
Of life reborn in every hue.

Emerging flowers stretch and bloom,
Beneath the skies' consuming gloom.
The earth awakens, fresh and bright,
In the embrace of nature's might.

No fear remains in the curtain's fall,
For through the deluge, we find our call.
In unity, we face the storm,
Embracing all that keeps us warm.

Symphony of Sighs

In quiet corners where shadows blend,
A symphony of sighs begins to mend.
Whispers linger beneath the moon,
Stories shared, as if in tune.

Each breath a note, each glance a line,
In this melody, our hearts entwine.
Gentle echoes of what once was,
Carried softly, because it does.

The night unveils its tender grace,
As stars weave light in a passionate embrace.
Ghosts of laughter float in the air,
A haunting song of love and care.

With every sigh, a memory fades,
Yet still in silence, hope invades.
We find ourselves in twilight's glow,
In the symphony of all we know.

So let us sigh through joy and pain,
For each has beauty, like falling rain.
In every moment, a chance to feel,
In this harmony, our hearts heal.

Confluence of Water and Earth

Rivers weave through land's embrace,
Mingling currents, a gentle trace.
Bringing life to fields so wide,
Nature's pulse, the earth's heartbeat inside.

Mountains bow to the flowing tide,
In harmony, worlds collide.
Mist rises where water flows,
A dance of elements, nature's prose.

Pebbles whisper tales of time,
Echoing in rhythm, a subtle rhyme.
Roots find solace in wet clay,
Bound together, come what may.

Colors bloom along the shore,
Life awakens, forevermore.
In stillness, secrets wait to unfurl,
The confluence dances, a timeless whirl.

As daylight kisses dusk's embrace,
The union glows in twilight's grace.
Footsteps meet at the water's edge,
A pledge of balance, nature's hedge.

Unexpected Canopies

Beneath the leaves of emerald sheen,
Whispers of secrets lie unseen.
Branches cradle hidden nests,
Life unfurling in quiet quests.

Sunlight dances through the green,
A patchwork quilt, a serene scene.
Beckoning creatures small and shy,
In shade where dreams and shadows lie.

Vines embrace the ancient bark,
Nature's art in every mark.
Fruits dangle low, ripe and sweet,
A feast awaits where earth and sky meet.

Clouds weave stories in the air,
Drifting softly without a care.
Rustling leaves join the song,
In trails where wanderers belong.

A world alive, vibrant, and vast,
Under canopies built to last.
Nature's embrace, a gentle call,
In unexpected spaces, we find it all.

Breath of the Earth

Inhale the dawn, the earth awakes,
With gentle sighs, the stillness breaks.
Mountains rise in quiet grace,
Holding secrets in their face.

Forests hum an ancient tune,
As rivers glimmer beneath the moon.
Each leaf speaks, each stone replies,
In harmony where silence lies.

Wind carries whispers from afar,
Tickling petals of the flowered spar.
Roots dive deep, seeking embrace,
Life's foundation in every space.

In the dusk, a heartbeat thunders,
As shadows stretch and light encumbers.
Breath of the earth, an endless song,
In cycles vast, where all belong.

Feel the pulse, the thrum, the beat,
In every path, our journey's fleet.
Nature calls in tender tones,
A symphony where life intones.

Harmonies of the Thunder

In tempest's roar, the skies collide,
Nature's voice cannot hide.
Lightning dances, bold and bright,
Scribing stories across the night.

Raindrops mold the thirsty ground,
Each droplet sings, a soothing sound.
Echoes of the storm arise,
In the clash of nature's cries.

Mountains tremble at the call,
As shadows loom, the thunderball.
In wild rhythm, winds entwine,
A symphony of earth's design.

After the storm, a silence swells,
Whispers linger, nature dwells.
Sunlight breaks, the world anew,
Painting skies in vibrant hue.

Feel the pulse of the driving rain,
A melody that binds our pain.
In every heart, a spark ignites,
The harmonies of stormy nights.

Porter of Peaceful Interludes

In quiet corners where shadows creep,
A gentle whisper lulls the deep.
The sun dips low, the world sighs slow,
A moment's peace, a tranquil glow.

Through winding paths where breezes play,
The busy minds find time to sway.
The heartbeats soften, fears dissolve,
In sacred stillness, souls evolve.

Each fleeting hour, a treasure sought,
In simple joys, we find our thought.
A laugh, a glance, a shared embrace,
In every pause, we find our grace.

The stars above begin to gleam,
As tranquil waters weave a dream.
A porter waits with open arms,
To gift the night its soothing charms.

So linger here, where silence reigns,
Where joy and peace erase the pains.
In this retreat, let echoes cease,
And find within, your heart's own peace.

The Calm After the Fury

When thunder roars and darkness spills,
The heart beats fast, the spirit chills.
Yet through the storm, hope starts to glow,
In whispered breaths, the calm will grow.

The raindrops dance on windowpanes,
Each splatter sings of sweet refrains.
As skies unveil their azure hues,
The earth awakes, the soul renews.

Soft breezes weave through fallen leaves,
A gentle touch, the spirit cleaves.
In quiet moments, fear takes flight,
And dawn unfolds, embracing light.

We gather strength from nature's grace,
Resilience shines upon our face.
For after storms, we rise anew,
In calmness wrapped, we find our view.

The echoes fade, our hearts align,
In tranquil space, our hopes entwine.
A promise made, to face the day,
With courage strong, we find our way.

A Tender Kiss from Above

A gentle breeze flows through the trees,
Caressing leaves with whispered ease.
In dawn's embrace, the sun will rise,
And greet the world with softest sighs.

The stars that twinkled through the night,
Still hold the magic of their light.
With every ray that warms the ground,
A tender kiss of love is found.

The blossoms bloom in perfect time,
Their colors dance, a sweet sublime.
Each petal sings a love so true,
A testimony, fresh and new.

When shadows loom and hope feels far,
Look to the sky, your guiding star.
For in the heavens, love will shine,
A tender kiss, forever thine.

Embrace the warmth, let worries cease,
In every moment, find your peace.
As day unfolds and dreams arise,
A tender kiss, our hearts in ties.

Chasing Rainbows' Shadows

In skies of gray where dreams take flight,
We chase the rainbows, seeking light.
With every storm that draws us near,
A splash of colors, bright and clear.

The hills and valleys, vast and wide,
Hold stories waiting to confide.
Each hue a promise, bold and bright,
A pathway traced in pure delight.

Through misty veils and sunlit beams,
We find the joy in whispered dreams.
As laughter echoes, spirits soar,
In every shadow, we want more.

The journey calls, we take the chance,
To dance with fate, to dream, to prance.
With open hearts, we roam the land,
In search of rainbows, hand in hand.

For life's a quest, a vibrant game,
With every step, we find our aim.
And as we chase, we come to see,
In shadows danced, we're truly free.

Threads of Pearls from Heaven

In the sky, soft whispers glow,
Threads of pearls begin to flow,
Falling gently, a sacred gift,
Nature's grace, a heart to lift.

Each droplet holds a silent wish,
Woven dreams in every swish,
A tapestry of light and air,
A moment's pause, a breath laid bare.

Twinkling bright against the dark,
Shimmers where the wishes spark,
A dance of hope, a fleeting chance,
Together, all in nature's dance.

Golden rays through openings shine,
Painting paths, a soft design,
As the world slows down in awe,
Threads of pearls, a joyful draw.

Embrace the magic, let it reign,
Through the joy, through the pain,
In the quiet, find your song,
Threads of pearls, where hearts belong.

Wind-Kissed Raindrops

Raindrops fall from clouded skies,
Kissed by winds, like gentle sighs,
Each one dancing on the street,
Nature's rhythm, soft and sweet.

Listen closely to their song,
Whispers of the earth, so long,
Echoes in the puddles found,
Beauty in the world around.

A silver veil wraps the day,
Colors blend in grand ballet,
Life awakens with every spark,
Softened air, elusive hark.

In the breeze, a story flows,
Secrets held, the garden knows,
Every drop a story told,
A treasure bright, a charm of gold.

As the sun begins to peek,
Raindrops shimmer, soft and meek,
A gentle kiss, a love remade,
In the dance of light and shade.

The Quiet After the Thunder

When thunder falls and shadows play,
The world holds breath, then drifts away,
Silence blankets, soft and deep,
In this hush, the memories seep.

Raindrops linger on grass tips,
Nature rests from stormy sips,
Pulsing life in peace and grace,
Calming whispers in this space.

The air is fresh, the sky laid bare,
A canvas washed in love and care,
A moment captured, quiet claims,
The echo of old love's names.

In this pause, our spirits soar,
Unraveled thoughts begin to pour,
Finding solace in the still,
A quiet heart, a tranquil will.

From the chaos, hope is spun,
A gentle start beneath the sun,
Life unfolds with fragrant dreams,
In the quiet, love redeems.

Dreams in a Deluge

In tempest's heart, a dream ignites,
Floating through tumultuous nights,
In every storm, a vision clear,
Woven paths drawing us near.

Raindrops pour like whispered fates,
As the wind through branches crates,
Every splash, a promise told,
In the chaos, dreams unfold.

Underneath the drumming sky,
Hope takes wing, it flutters high,
With every flash, a chance to see,
Fleeting moments setting free.

In deluge, we find our light,
Guided by fierce, sparkled might,
Even as the shadows loom,
A world reborn, in bright bloom.

So let the rains pour down with grace,
Every drop a soft embrace,
In dreams unleashed, the heart will roam,
In the deluge, we find home.

Forgotten Traces in the Fog

Whispers dance on the cool air,
Footprints fade without a care.
Shadows linger, soft and pale,
Secrets hidden, dreams set sail.

The world feels lost in a mist,
Paths obscure, chance dismissed.
Echoes murmur, tales unsaid,
In the silence, memories tread.

Voices call from the depths of glen,
Fleeting moments, lost again.
Time rolls on, though we can't see,
The fog conceals what's meant to be.

Yet in the haze, a spark ignites,
Old hopes flutter, taking flight.
We grasp at shadows, fleeting trails,
In the stillness, the heart unveils.

And when the sun breaks through the gray,
Forgotten traces drift away.
Yet still they linger in our mind,
The paths we walk, all intertwined.

Clouded Reveries

Drifting thoughts in a muted sky,
Softened edges as moments fly.
Memories wrapped in a gentle shroud,
Whispers linger in dream's soft crowd.

Cascading colors blurred with time,
Melodies swirl, an unchained rhyme.
Thoughts entwined like vines that climb,
In this hazy realm, we find the sublime.

Glances exchanged in twilight's haze,
Caught in a dance of shadowed rays.
Unraveled dreams and fleeting sighs,
Where every whisper softly lies.

Moments held in the heart's embrace,
Lingering scents of a distant place.
Clouded reveries take their flight,
Chasing stars through the endless night.

And as we wander through the fog,
With every tear and every cog,
We gather shards of time, so sweet,
In clouded reveries, our minds complete.

The Tenderness of Sudden Showers

Raindrops kiss the thirsty ground,
Soft pitter-patter, a soothing sound.
Clouds embrace in a lover's sigh,
Nature weeps as the sun waves goodbye.

Each drop a story, a longing told,
In fleeting moments, the world turns bold.
They dance on petals, a tender grace,
Transforming all with their gentle pace.

Silhouettes shrouded in misty light,
Hearts awaken under soft twilight.
The scent of earth in the cooling air,
Sudden showers paint the world with care.

Songs of droplets, a timeless tune,
A serenade beneath the moon.
In every splash, life finds release,
The tenderness of nature's peace.

After the storm, a rainbow gleams,
Casting hopes in familiar dreams.
Life renews with every pass,
In sudden showers, we find our grass.

Hushed Moments Under Shelter

Beneath the roof, the world slows down,
Raindrops tap gently, a calming sound.
We sit in shadows, holding tight,
In hushed moments, hearts ignite.

Candles flicker with whispers low,
Stories woven in amber glow.
Soft laughter dances in the air,
In this shelter, we're free from care.

Outside, the tempest finds its voice,
Inside, we revel in our choice.
Fleeting time wraps us in warm fold,
Memories crafted, hearts unfold.

The world may rage, but here, we stay,
In hushed moments, come what may.
Each heartbeat echoes, tender and clear,
In the sanctuary, nothing to fear.

And when the storm begins to fade,
We cherish the kindness that we made.
Hushed moments linger, warm as sun,
Under shelter, two souls become one.

The Serenity between Raindrops

In quiet moments, raindrops fall,
A gentle rhythm, nature's call.
Each drop a whisper, soft and clear,
In this embrace, we feel no fear.

Among the trees, a dance begins,
Leaves twirl softly in the winds.
The air, so fresh, like new-born sighs,
Holds promises of brighter skies.

Puddles form like mirror dreams,
Reflecting hopes, or so it seems.
With every splash, the world ignites,
A tapestry of pure delights.

In the stillness after rain,
Life awakens, sheds its pain.
Colors vibrant, spirits lift,
Nature's solace, a perfect gift.

So let us cherish each brief pause,
In raindrops, find life's hidden laws.
A tranquil heart can always see,
The beauty in simplicity.

Lullabies of Nature's Tears

When raindrops weep for skies above,
They sing a song, a tale of love.
Each tear that falls, a tender grace,
Cradling earth in soft embrace.

Beneath the clouds, the flowers sway,
In rhythm with the skies' ballet.
Nature hums a soothing tune,
As droplets dance beneath the moon.

The gentle hush after the storm,
Brings forth whispers, fresh and warm.
Every heartbeat, every sigh,
Nature's lullabies soaring high.

In these moments, calm and sweet,
The world finds rest, a slow heartbeat.
As tears from heaven blend with light,
Hope rekindled, shining bright.

So listen close, to every drop,
A melody, we can't stop.
In nature's tears, we find our way,
A symphony that guides our day.

Veiled Comforts

In twilight hours, the shadows blend,
Whispers of night, as day will end.
Veils of mist wrap around each tree,
A cloak of peace, for you and me.

The stars peek through with twinkling eyes,
Sharing secrets of moonlit skies.
Each breath of wind, a soothing balm,
In this space, we find our calm.

Softly glowing lanterns ignite,
Illuminating paths of light.
Every corner, a hidden gem,
Nature's gifts, we can condemn.

As darkness dances, shadows play,
Veiled comforts guide us on our way.
In stillness, hearts begin to heal,
Embracing all that we can feel.

So let us wander, hand in hand,
Through veils of night, across the land.
With every step, a tale unfolds,
In whispered dreams, our truth beholds.

Pieces of Skyfall

From above, the heavens weep,
Droplets fall, secrets to keep.
Each piece of sky, a story's thread,
Tales of the life that lies ahead.

As puddles gather, stories grow,
Reflecting dreams that softly flow.
Ripples dance in harmony,
A canvas of tranquility.

In every drop, the sun will hide,
Waiting for the clouds to guide.
Hope shines bright in every tear,
Painting pictures, crystal clear.

With every storm, a new beginning,
Life reborn, the heart is singing.
Pieces of sky, like hearts entwined,
In the chaos, love defined.

So gather these drops, hold them near,
Fragments of joy, whispers sincere.
In every rain, a chance to see,
The beauty that sets our spirits free.

A Shelter from Turbulence

In the eye of the storm's fierce embrace,
We find a calm, a sacred space.
Where shadows dance with fleeting light,
A refuge blooms in darkest night.

Whispers of winds, a gentle sigh,
Cradle us as the tempest flies.
Each droplet sings a melody,
Of peace beneath the wailing sea.

Branches bend, but do not break,
In nature's hold, our fears forsake.
Roots deep in earth, steadfast and strong,
We weather the storm, where we belong.

The sky may roar, the waves may clash,
Yet here we stand, earth's vibrant stash.
Amidst the chaos, hearts aligned,
We seek the shelter, love defined.

So let the lightning strike and spark,
For in the dark, we find our mark.
Together we brave the savage night,
In unity, we find our light.

The Heartbeat of the Storm

Thunder rumbles, a mighty growl,
The heavens weep with a solemn howl.
Each drop a beat in nature's song,
A rhythm fierce, relentless, strong.

Clouds converge, a swirling dance,
Nature's fury, a wild romance.
Yet in this chaos, hearts align,
In tempest's pulse, our souls entwine.

With every flash, the sky ignites,
A heart awakens, fierce delights.
In the storm's embrace, we find our way,
Guided by the night to break the day.

Torrents pour, and winds may bend,
Yet in this storm, we shall transcend.
The heartbeat thrums beneath our feet,
In every surge, our courage meets.

For storms remind us, we are alive,
In turbulent seas, we learn to thrive.
Together we dance in nature's grace,
Finding solace in the storm's embrace.

The Gift of the Drench

Rain falls softly, a tender kiss,
Each droplet whispers of sweet bliss.
A gift unwrapped from skies above,
Nurturing Earth with endless love.

Puddles gather, reflections gleam,
In every drop, the world may dream.
Life awakens, colors bright,
Underneath the drench, pure delight.

Fields adorned in glittering dew,
Nature's palette, a vibrant hue.
Crickets chirp, the frogs rejoice,
In the wet embrace, the world finds voice.

From rooftops, streams begin to flow,
Washing the dust where the wildflowers grow.
Embracing each drop as a sacred bond,
In the gift of rain, our hearts respond.

So let it pour, let the rivers rise,
For in the rain, pure magic lies.
Together we dance in the gentle drench,
Finding our place on Earth's great bench.

when the Earth Breathes

Beneath the sky, the Earth exhales,
In whispered secrets, nature trails.
Each sigh a promise, every breeze,
A tender pulse among the trees.

Mountains rise, their shadows cast,
In harmony, they hold the past.
When leaves unfurl, the air ignites,
The Earth awakens, magic ignites.

In morning light, the flowers bloom,
With each inhale, dispelling gloom.
The roots embrace, the branches reach,
In perfect balance, life they teach.

When seasons shift, the world shall change,
Yet in its core, love's never strange.
A symphony of colors weaves,
As nature breathes, our spirit cleaves.

So take a moment, pause and feel,
The sacred rhythms, nature's reel.
When the Earth breathes, we too align,
Finding in every moment, the divine.

Whispers of the Falling Sky

Softly the clouds begin to weep,
Their tears like silver, secrets keep.
Through the air, a gentle sigh,
Wrapped in the whispers of the sky.

Drifting leaves dance in the breeze,
Nature's message, a rustling tease.
Moments fleeting, time slips by,
Caught in the whispers of the sky.

Raindrops kiss the thirsty ground,
With each note, a symphony found.
In cool embrace, the world awry,
Listening close, the falling sky.

Birds take flight on wings of grace,
Chasing echoes in the open space.
Carved in hues of deepening dye,
Dreams float softly from the sky.

Stars emerge as daylight ends,
Secrets shared, the night descends.
In the stillness, hearts comply,
With the final whispers of the sky.

Tears of the Earth

The soil breathes a heavy sigh,
Underneath the endless sky.
Mountains cradle every tear,
Whispers echo, soft and clear.

Rivers surge with heartfelt pain,
Carving paths through joy and rain.
Each drop sings of love gone dry,
Softly, the tears of the earth fly.

Flowers bloom despite the ache,
Colorful dreams that never break.
In meadows vast, where shadows lie,
Hope arises from tears nearby.

Silent forests hold their breath,
Worn by ages, faced with death.
Yet life pushes forth to try,
Healing scars with tears held high.

In every storm, a lesson learned,
From ashes rise, the world has turned.
From darkness comes the light to pry,
Life renewed through the earth's tears dry.

The Symphony of Drizzle

A pitter-patter on the ground,
A gentle rhythm, peace is found.
Each drop a note, soft and shy,
Playing the tune of the drizzle's sigh.

Windows fog and moments freeze,
Wrapped in the warmth, a subtle tease.
Caught in dreams where raindrops lie,
Carried softly as the drizzles fly.

City streets wear shining coats,
Reflecting stories in small boats.
With every droplet, hopes amplify,
Melodies weave through the drizzle's cry.

Children splash in puddles wide,
Bounce of joy, they run and glide.
In laughter and play, spirits high,
Dancing freely in the drizzle's sky.

When the sun breaks through the gray,
Moments cherished, dreams at play.
With every storm, a gift awry,
Love's sweet song in the drizzle's sigh.

Echoes in the Gloom

In shadows deep where silence grows,
Whispers linger, soft and slow.
The heart beats in a muted tune,
Melancholy wrapped in the gloom.

Footsteps fade on cobbled streets,
Lost in echoes where memory meets.
The past haunts beneath the moon,
Shadows dance in the gentle gloom.

Clouds gather like forgotten dreams,
A tapestry of muted seams.
Through stillness, strength begins to bloom,
Braving all within the gloom.

Voices murmur, secrets shared,
In the darkness, none prepared.
Hope flickers, a fire's plume,
Sparking life amidst the gloom.

Yet dawn arrives with colors bright,
Chasing away the lingering night.
With every step, the heart anew,
Emerging bold from whispers' rue.

Grains of Hope from the Heavens

In the fields, seeds rest,
Under skies, promises bloom,
Each drop of rain a gift,
Whispering dreams to the earth.

Morning light breaks through,
Chasing shadows of the night,
Gentle winds carry tales,
Of hope rising with the sun.

Roots entwine in the soil,
Drawing strength from deep within,
With every heartbeat of life,
A tapestry of potential.

In silence, they await,
The dance of time and fate,
For in patience, they know,
The embrace of fruitful days.

Grains of hope, so tender,
Growing tall against the storm,
They remind us of our strength,
To push forward, to transform.

The Charms of Clouded Days

Gray blankets drape the sky,
Not a hint of sunlight's glow,
A quiet charm in stillness,
Where secrets softly sow.

Winds whisper through the trees,
In gentle, playful sighs,
Each branch sways with a story,
Of dreams that never die.

Raindrops dance on petals,
An orchestra of the divine,
Each splash a verse of beauty,
In nature's grand design.

The world feels wrapped in hush,
As if time pauses to breathe,
With clouded hues enchanting,
From our worries we can cleave.

Find solace in the gray,
In moods that ebb and flow,
Embrace the charms of days,
When life's colors fade to slow.

Liquid Lullabies

A stream flows, soft and clear,
Whispers secrets to the trees,
With every splash, a story,
Carried on a gentle breeze.

Moonlight glimmers on the waves,
As night wraps the world in peace,
Each ripple sings a lullaby,
Where all thoughts find their release.

Stars reflect in tranquil pools,
Mirroring the dreams we hold,
A canvas painted with hopes,
In liquid silver and gold.

Close your eyes and listen deep,
To the songs that nature weaves,
For in the heart of water,
Lie the dreams that night believes.

Let the melodies embrace,
Drown your worries in the flow,
Liquid lullabies will hold,
All the wishes we let go.

In the Wake of Thunder

Dark clouds gather with a roar,
Nature's pulse begins to race,
Lightning flashes through the night,
Marking time and space.

The earth shakes with rumbling might,
A primal symphony unfolds,
In the wake of thunder's sound,
Ancient stories yet untold.

Raindrops drum on rooftops' skin,
A rhythm fierce, a wild dance,
Every clap a heartbeat's call,
Inviting us to take a chance.

With each echo, fears subside,
As courage rises with the storm,
For in chaos, strength is found,
And hearts begin to warm.

When the tempest fades away,
The world is washed anew,
In the wake of roaring storms,
Hope ignites, bright and true.

Fragmented Moments Beneath a Gloomy Canopy

Under shadows dark and deep,
Memories flutter, then they seep.
In the silence, whispers dwell,
Stories tangled, hard to tell.

Branches reach with outstretched hands,
Life unfolds in distant lands.
Each step taken, a choice made,
In these fragments, dreams cascade.

A soft rain begins to fall,
Echoes dance; they know it all.
Through the mist, we seek the light,
In this gloom, we find our sight.

Time drips down like fragile dew,
Moments fade, yet feel so true.
Beneath this canopy of gray,
Hope lingers; it won't stray.

Hold these moments, let them guide,
In their beauty, let us bide.
Though they're fleeting, they remain,
In our hearts, they conquer pain.

The Language of Drenched Leaves

Whispers flutter on the breeze,
Stories danced beneath the trees.
Each drop tells a tale of grace,
Nature's hymn in every space.

Drenched leaves glisten, soft and bright,
In the shadows, there's a light.
Every rustle speaks in tunes,
Beneath the weeping afternoon.

Colors shift, a vibrant show,
In the rain, their hues will glow.
Each leaf tells a secret song,
In this symphony, we belong.

Listen close, the world reveals,
Through wet whispers, truth conceals.
Nature's language, pure and clear,
In every droplet, draw us near.

Embrace the whispers of the trees,
Find the solace in the breeze.
Drenched leaves hold a timeless lore,
In their beauty, we explore.

A Canvas of Glistening Pearls

Morning light on crested waves,
Nature's art, the heart it saves.
Each droplet reflects a tale,
A shimmering, soft-spoken veil.

On the shore where sea meets sand,
Treasures glimmer, gently planned.
Pearls of wisdom, scattered, bright,
In the sun, they dance with light.

A canvas wrought with silver dreams,
Whispers float on lapping streams.
Each pearl holds a memory's kiss,
In their beauty, find your bliss.

Softly cradled in the tide,
In their magic, we confide.
Nature's brush strokes, bold yet sweet,
A canvas where our hearts once meet.

Glistening pearls beneath the sky,
With each wave, we dare to fly.
In this moment, life unfurls,
A canvas rich with glistening pearls.

Hushed Conversations with the Wind

In twilight's glow, the whispers start,
The wind carries a tender heart.
Leaves respond with soft replies,
In their dance, the spirit flies.

Hushed conversations, secrets shared,
Between the trees, we are ensnared.
Breezes weave through every thought,
In their grip, we are caught.

Listen close, the night unfolds,
Stories wrapped in gentle holds.
Through the branches, voices blend,
A melody that seems to mend.

With every sigh, a truth is spun,
In the stillness, we are one.
Intertwined in nature's care,
In hushed moments, feelings bare.

Embrace the whispers, let them soar,
In this softness, find your core.
Conversations with the afterglow,
In the wind, let your spirit flow.

The Beauty of Drenched Earth

The rain has fallen soft and clear,
Awakening life, the scent of cheer.
Each droplet weaves a coat of green,
In nature's hug, the world is clean.

Puddles gleam like mirrored skies,
Reflecting dreams where beauty lies.
Flowers dance, their colors bold,
In a quilt of life, a story told.

The soil, rich with whispered cries,
Nurtures roots where courage lies.
In every heart, a seed is sown,
From drenched earth, our strength has grown.

Every leaf, a tale of grace,
Emerald gems in nature's embrace.
The beauty shines in every part,
Awakening joy within the heart.

Serenity Within a Peal

The bell's soft toll rides on the breeze,
A melody that brings us peace.
Each note descends like gentle rain,
A balm for all our hidden pain.

In stillness, echoes of the past,
Remind us moments never last.
With each peal, a breath we take,
A pause in time for our hearts' sake.

A quiet space, a sanctuary,
Where thoughts can drift, and spirits free.
In every chime, the world retreats,
Embraced in calm, where wonder meets.

The fading sound, so soft and slight,
Leaves traces of the purest light.
In every heart, a whisper grows,
A sense of peace that gently flows.

Curtain of Clouds

A curtain drawn across the sky,
Soft whispers of a breeze slip by.
The sun peeks through with gentle grace,
Illuminating nature's face.

Clouds drift slowly, a dance above,
Wrapping earth in a veil of love.
In shades of gray and silver bright,
They bring the day its soothing light.

Each swirl and fold a story spun,
In twilight's grip, when day is done.
The horizon blurs with colors bold,
As soft twilight begins to unfold.

Beyond the curtain, dreams abound,
In whispered hopes, true joy is found.
Nature's heart beats strong and free,
In each soft cloud, a memory.

Tranquility's Cascade

A waterfall cascades with grace,
Filling the air with nature's face.
Each drop a note in harmony,
Creating calm for you and me.

The sound of water, a gentle hymn,
A journey where our souls can swim.
In sparkling streams, reflections gleam,
We find our truths in nature's dream.

The rocks are worn, but stand so tall,
Guardians of peace, that beckon all.
Within their arms, we pause to breathe,
In their embrace, we learn to believe.

As mist envelops, dreams arise,
Soft whispers linger in the skies.
In every drop, a story flows,
Tranquility's heart forever glows.

The Gentle Touch of Water

Rippling softly, a stream flows,
Whispers of calm on the shore's prose.
Gentle caress on sunlit rocks,
Nature's tender touch, it unlocks.

Dew-kissed petals in morning's light,
Each drop a gem, a pure delight.
Cool breeze dances through the trees,
A soothing hymn, a tranquil tease.

Waves lap gently, a rhythmic song,
Inviting hearts to sing along.
In its embrace, all worries fade,
A peaceful realm, where dreams are made.

Crystalline pools reflect the sky,
Where laughter echoes and spirits fly.
In the hush of dusk, stillness reigns,
The gentle touch of water remains.

Endless cycles of ebb and flow,
Nature's promise in every glow.
In its depths, a world so vast,
The gentle touch, a spell cast.

Melodies of a Soggy Evening

Raindrops tap on window panes,
Nature sings in soft refrains.
Clouds embrace the twilight glow,
Melodies of a night in flow.

Puddles mirror the fading light,
Each ripple tells a tale of night.
Wind whispers secrets in the trees,
A soggy serenade on the breeze.

Footsteps echo on dampened ground,
In the hush, pure magic is found.
A symphony of water's dance,
In shadows, dreams find their chance.

Glistening streets wear a shiny coat,
Voices mingle, a gentle note.
In the glow of streetlamp grace,
A soggy evening's warm embrace.

As laughter blends with falling rain,
This melody lingers, sweet refrain.
With every drop, a story's spun,
A symphony shared, as day is done.

Nature's Soft Embrace

In a meadow where daisies sway,
Sunlight kisses the blooms in play.
Butterflies flutter without a care,
Nature's softness fills the air.

Whispers of wind through ancient trees,
A calming balm, a gentle breeze.
Petals fall like dreams on the ground,
In this embrace, true peace is found.

Sunsets paint the sky in hues,
Crimson, gold, and calming blues.
Horizon glows, a soft caress,
In nature's arms, we find our rest.

Streams weave tales of time and space,
Lap by lap, they find their place.
Every ripple tells a tale,
Of nature's love that cannot fail.

With every dawn, a chance to see,
How soft the world can truly be.
In every moment, peace can trace,
Its path in nature's soft embrace.

The Gray Canvas Above

Clouds gather in a painter's stroke,
A canvas gray, where shadows poke.
Hints of silver, whispers of white,
A masterpiece in fading light.

Raindrops fall like artists' tears,
Drumming softly, calming fears.
Each drop a note in nature's tune,
A symphony beneath the moon.

The gray unfurls, a cloak so vast,
In its embrace, all chaos cast.
Softening edges of day's sharp light,
This gentle shroud, a cozy night.

Birdsongs hush as the shadows creep,
In the gray, the world will sleep.
A lullaby of drifting stars,
Connecting dreams in midnight bars.

As the canvas shifts and sways,
In muted tones, the night plays.
The gray invites each heart to pause,
In its stillness, we find our cause.

Tranquility of the Saturated Ground

Beneath a sky of muted grey,
The earth sighs softly, soaked in rain.
Roots drink deep, in silent sway,
Life awakens, free from pain.

A quiet whisper, nature's song,
Moss carpets stones, lush and bright.
In this haven, we belong,
With each droplet, pure delight.

Birds call gently from the trees,
Dancing leaves in soft embrace.
A breath of wind, a fragrant breeze,
In the stillness, we find grace.

Reflections gleam on puddled ground,
Mirrors of a world anew.
In each ripple, peace is found,
In this moment, hearts construe.

The saturated ground holds sway,
With every heartbeat, nature's sound.
In this realm, we wish to stay,
Tranquility, forever crowned.

Dappled Light Through Mist

Morning breaks with golden gleam,
Light dances through the shrouded haze.
A softened world, a fleeting dream,
Where shadows play in gentle plays.

Leaves adorned with drops of dew,
Twinkling gems in the sunlight's kiss.
In this realm, serenity grew,
Every glance holds a tranquil bliss.

Rays cut through the lingering fog,
Whispers of dawn, a beckoning call.
Nature wraps, a dreamy smog,
In stillness, we are captivated all.

Pathways beckon, secrets lie,
Under archways of tender green.
Each step taken, we learn to fly,
In the mist, our spirits sheen.

Through dappled light, the world awakes,
As hearts align with nature's grace.
A canvas painted, beauty makes,
In the embrace, we find our place.

The Quietude after the Downpour

Pavements glisten, washed anew,
Gentle silence fills the air.
Nature breathes, a tranquil view,
In solitude, we lay bare.

Leaves whisper tales of the night,
Each droplet tells of love's sweet pain.
In the calm, we find respite,
Healing in the soft refrain.

Clouds part gently, revealing blue,
A canvas cleared, the sun shines bright.
With every glimpse, rebirth feels true,
Hope springs forth from out of sight.

Birds return with joyful cheer,
Flutters echo in the still.
In the quiet, hearts draw near,
Listening to the world's goodwill.

The downpour fades, yet magic stays,
In crispness lingers, pure and deep.
Through quietude, we find our ways,
In every heart, a promise to keep.

Horizon's Embrace

The sun dips low, a fiery hue,
Kissed by oceans, painted skies.
In twilight's glow, dreams renew,
As day surrenders, no goodbyes.

Waves whisper softly, secrets told,
On the shore, they ebb and flow.
Golden light, a sight to behold,
Embracing night with a gentle glow.

Stars emerge, a scattered seed,
In the calm of the coming night.
In the darkness, hearts are freed,
Chasing dreams, welcoming light.

Each horizon holds a promise,
Of tomorrow's warmth and grace.
In each sunset, a soft solace,
As shadows dance in a soft embrace.

With every breath, we feel the space,
Of what has been and what will be.
In this moment, find your place,
To gaze upon the endless sea.

Serene Currents

Gentle ripples kiss the shore,
Whispers of water, forevermore,
In quiet depths, secrets lie,
Beneath the vast, embracing sky.

Leaves sway softly in the breeze,
Nature dances with such ease,
Sunlight glistens on the stream,
Life unfolds like a sweet dream.

Frogs croak out their evening song,
Echoes in the twilight long,
Reflections shimmer, gold and grey,
As dusk turns into night from day.

Stars begin their nightly rise,
Painting patterns in the skies,
The moonlight wraps the world in peace,
In every heart, a gentle cease.

Nature hums a lullaby,
As the currents quietly sigh,
In the calm of night's embrace,
The world finds its sacred space.

A Tapestry of Tears

Tears of sorrow weave their path,
A tapestry of pain and wrath,
Each drop falls with a heavy heart,
In silence, they craft a work of art.

Moments lost, like threads undone,
A quilt of memories spun in sun,
Faded smiles, shadows remain,
Bound in the fabric of our pain.

Stitches of laughter intertwined,
In the fabric, hope we find,
With every tear, a tale is spun,
A reminder of battles fought and won.

Yet beyond the woven grief,
Lies a thread of sweet relief,
Through the dark, new colors rise,
Painting the world with brighter skies.

In this tapestry, life flows true,
Woven dark and woven blue,
Each tear, a testament of soul,
A story whispered, making whole.

Soothing the Parched Earth

Cracked and dry, the ground does plead,
Beneath the sun's relentless heat,
A whisper of rain, a tender sigh,
Promising life from the open sky.

Drops begin to fall like balm,
Nourishing the earth with soothing calm,
Each splash holds a silent prayer,
Reviving colors, vibrant and rare.

Flowers bloom in bursts of cheer,
As nature bathes in waters clear,
Grasses stretch with newfound grace,
In every droplet, a warm embrace.

Streams awaken, laughter flows,
As joy in every corner grows,
Puddles gleam like mirrors bright,
Reflecting praises for the night.

Though seasons shift and change their pace,
The earth remains a sacred place,
Where every droplet tells a story,
Of hope renewed and nature's glory.

The Embrace of Evening Drizzle

A gentle mist begins to fall,
Whispers soft, a velvet call,
The world adorned in silken grey,
As twilight ushers in the day.

Each drop dances, a fleeting sigh,
Caressing earth as shadows lie,
A tender kiss upon the street,
Where puddles gather, cold and sweet.

The air, it sings of fresh delight,
As stars appear, flickers of light,
In the hush, the heart finds ease,
Wrapped in warmth of evening's breeze.

Underneath the dripping trees,
The world exhales, a sigh of peace,
Each heartbeat matches nature's rhyme,
In this embrace, we lose all time.

So let the drizzle fall and play,
A melody for the end of day,
In every drop, a story flows,
As evening's gentle beauty grows.

The Sighs of Saturated Air

In the whispering dusk, soft shadows play,
Heavy clouds linger, reluctant to sway.
Raindrops murmur on pavement below,
Each sigh a story, the earth's gentle woe.

Breath of the trees, soaked in the night,
Nature's embrace, a soothing, sweet light.
The scent of the rain, fresh and so clear,
Holds tender memories that draw us near.

Echoes of thunder, a deep, rolling din,
The heart of the storm beats quietly within.
Saturated air, where all secrets reside,
In the calm of the tempest, all fears can hide.

Whispers of longing in every small gust,
The world breathes anew, in silence we trust.
As droplets connect, like threads in a weave,
In the sighs of the air, we learn to believe.

Once Upon a Deluge

Once upon a deluge, the rivers awoke,
With laughter and splashes, their joy bespoke.
Clouds gathered thick, weaving tales in the sky,
As nature rejoiced, no heart left to dry.

The rooftops glistened, a shimmering dance,
Waterfalls streamed down, in a wild romance.
Every puddle formed, a world of its own,
Reflecting the dreams that the raindrops had sown.

Children with paper boats, sailing through lanes,
In a kingdom of water, where magic remains.
Through laughter and lightning, the landscape transformed,
Once upon a deluge, where chaos conformed.

The echoes of thunder, the wind's gentle sigh,
A symphony played, beneath the gray sky.
And when the rain paused, the earth wore a crown,
Of diamonds and colors, in beauty renowned.

Consolation from Above

Waves of gold fall from the heavens' embrace,
In moments of stillness, we find our place.
Clouds drift like whispers, soft stories they tell,
Of solace and comfort, where shadows dwell.

As dusk settles down, the stars gently gleam,
A tapestry woven, a comforting dream.
Faint glimmers of hope dance on the horizon,
Each twinkle a promise, a new day to brighten.

The moon bathes the world in a silvery hue,
A calm reassurance in the darkness we view.
With each fleeting moment, we learn to let go,
Finding strength in the stillness, as night takes her bow.

Through whispers of wind, we hear the refrain,
Consolation from above, easing our pain.
In the quietest hours, tenderness flows,
A reminder that love in the shadows still grows.

The Art of Waterfall Sounds

In the heart of the forest, where stillness resides,
The art of waterfall sounds gently abides.
With whispers of splashes, the softest refrain,
Each droplet a note in the symphony's gain.

Peaceful the music, as echoes entwine,
A melody woven through branches and pine.
The rush of the current, like laughter sincere,
In the rhythm of water, the soul finds its cheer.

Sunbeams awaken the mist on the breeze,
Creating a canvas where troubles find ease.
Every rock a stage, every splash a grace,
Nature's ensemble in a timeless embrace.

The art of listening, a practiced refrain,
In the cadence of nature, we release our pain.
With the heart's quiet chorus, we learn to belong,
In the flowing serenity, we find our song.

Surrendering to Wetness

Raindrops dance on windowpanes,
Each one whispers a soft refrain,
Embracing earth with gentle grace,
In their touch, we find our place.

The world dissolves in muted hues,
As puddles form from endless dues,
We lose our breath in nature's sigh,
Beneath the clouds, our spirits fly.

Footsteps squelch on sodden ground,
Lost in moments, peace is found,
Every droplet a tale to share,
Awakening dreams in the cool air.

Wrapped in warmth of rain-soaked skies,
Tenderness within our eyes,
We surrender to the song,
Where wetness reigns, we all belong.

Let the current take us deep,
In the rhythm, secrets keep,
Surrendering to this embrace,
Finding solace in the space.

Threads of Nostalgia

Memories woven with gentle care,
Whispers of laughter linger in air,
Old photographs, corners worn,
In faded hues, our hearts are born.

Time's fabric stretches, threads entwined,
Moments cherished, love defined,
Every stitch a story told,
In every heart, a thread of gold.

Sunlit days and shadowed nights,
In quiet corners, soft delights,
Echoes of voices, sweet refrain,
The beauty held within the pain.

We weave our dreams with utmost grace,
Yet sometimes linger in the space,
Between what was and what will be,
Threads of nostalgia set us free.

Through tangled past, we wander slow,
Finding paths where memories flow,
In every heart, a timeless song,
Threads of nostalgia where we belong.

Echoing in Silver

Moonlight spills on tranquil streams,
Casting shadows, weaving dreams,
Whispers linger on the breeze,
In silver tones, our worries ease.

Stars ignite in velvet night,
Creating paths of purest light,
Every twinkle tells a tale,
In cosmic seas, we start to sail.

Reflections shimmer on the lake,
Mirroring thoughts that softly wake,
In every ripple, secrets dance,
Under the moon's mesmerizing trance.

Silence cradles ancient lore,
Lost in echoes, we explore,
In silver beams, a truth insists,
That night's embrace, we can't resist.

Through the darkness, hearts find grace,
The beauty in the stillness trace,
In every echo, love survives,
As silver light, our spirit thrives.

Softness Between the Drips

Gentle showers, nature sighs,
Blanketing earth where beauty lies,
Moments shared beneath the trees,
In droplets falling, we find peace.

Softness lingers on my skin,
Each refrain invites us in,
Caressing blooms in colors bright,
Transforming worlds with pure delight.

The air, a balm, the heart, a song,
In every drip, we feel we belong,
Whispers of joy in each cascade,
Nature's lullaby serenely played.

Dancing petals kiss the ground,
In every heartbeat, love is found,
We breathe in life's exquisite grace,
Lost in softness, we embrace.

Between the drips, a story weaves,
Of fleeting moments nature leaves,
In tender drops, our spirits lift,
Softness between, a precious gift.

When the Sky Weeps

Clouds gather thick in gray,
Raindrops dance upon the street.
Each droplet tells a tale,
Whispers soft, the heart's heartbeat.

In the hush, a world slows down,
Pavement glistens, life anew.
Every tear that falls with grace,
Cleansing soul, and washing blue.

A symphony of nature's tears,
Each splash sings of love and loss.
Underneath the somber skies,
There's beauty found in every gloss.

Lightning cracks, the thunder roars,
Nature's praise, a wild cheer.
Yet in the storm, a calm resides,
In the chaos, there's no fear.

When the sky weeps, hearts awake,
To the rhythm of the rain.
In the storm's embrace, we find,
A gentle peace amidst the pain.

Hidden Comfort in the Storm

The wind howls a fierce song,
Boughs bend, but do not break.
Nature's fury all around,
Yet, safety in the quake.

Within the chaos, warmth is found,
A heart beats close to mine.
Together, we brave the tempest,
With love that brightly shines.

Raindrops tap on windowpanes,
A melody, soft and sweet.
We hold tight, as shadows dance,
Finding solace, a rhythmic beat.

The world may toss, the world may churn,
But here we find our place.
In every gust and every strike,
There's hidden comfort, our embrace.

So when the storm may come to call,
We'll weather it with grace.
In the heart of wild and fierce,
We'll find our calm, our space.

The Lover's Mist

In twilight's gentle glow,
A mist rolls soft and thin.
Moments shared like whispered dreams,
Where love whispers within.

Shapes and shadows intertwine,
Fleeting glances, hearts aligned.
In the delicate embrace,
A world just for us designed.

Every breath, a promise made,
In silence, passions rise.
The fog wraps round like tender hands,
Softening all, removing lies.

With every turn and every sigh,
The air thick with sweet delight.
In the midst of heavy fog,
Our hearts soar, taking flight.

The mist conceals, then reveals,
In layers of soft embrace.
With love, the world feels lighter,
Lost forever in this space.

Calm Amidst Chaos

In the swirl of dance and noise,
Where shadows twist and spin,
A stillness blooms within my soul,
Peace rests where turmoil's been.

Worlds collide and tempests rage,
Yet here, I stand alone.
In the eye of every storm,
A tranquil heart is grown.

Voices clash like thunder's roar,
But within, a quiet spark.
It flickers softly, finding strength,
A lighthouse in the dark.

Here chaos loses sense of time,
As doubts begin to fade.
With calmness wrapped like a warm quilt,
True courage is displayed.

Though outside storms may threaten loud,
I find my steady ground.
In every whirlwind of my life,
A calmness, safe and sound.

The Cauldron of Refreshing Tides

Waves embrace the moonlit shore,
Bubbles rise with tales of yore.
Whispers carried by the breeze,
Nature's dance brings hearts at ease.

Salt and sun blend in delight,
mending souls beneath the light.
Tides that pull the burdens wide,
Cleansing dreams in rolling tide.

In this cauldron, spirits flow,
Washing worries, letting go.
Rhythms echo through the night,
Guiding hearts towards the light.

Each wave a whisper, soft and sweet,
Promises of love they meet.
As the stars begin to fade,
Purity in moonlit glade.

Finding solace in the spray,
Life reborn at break of day.
Cauldron glimmers, truths collide,
In its depths, we all abide.

Cascading Whispers

In the forest, secrets sigh,
Beneath the trees, where shadows lie.
Leaves are rustling in the air,
Echoing a timeless prayer.

Streams carving paths through stone,
Whispers share what we have known.
Softly tumbles water clear,
Carrying dreams of those held dear.

Softly spoken, nature's song,
In the twilight, where we belong.
Finding comfort in the flow,
Glimmers of the past we know.

Cascades trickle, wrapping round,
Every heartbeat is the sound.
Life a journey, swift or slow,
In the whispers, we shall grow.

Each descent a gentle grace,
In the shimmer, we find our place.
Tales of old, forever spin,
Cascading flows invite us in.

The Cleansing of Shadowed Streets

Raindrops fall on cobbled lanes,
Washing away the dust and stains.
As the city starts to gleam,
Hope revived, a waking dream.

Puddles mirror skies above,
Collecting stories, echoes of love.
Footsteps dance through midnight air,
Finding solace, no despair.

Shadows linger, softly fade,
In the light, the scars delayed.
Every drop a fresh new start,
Cleansing souls and mending hearts.

As dawn breaks, the light will bloom,
Erasing shadows, lifting gloom.
New beginnings on this street,
Where lost and found so often meet.

Cleansing rain and gentle sighs,
Life renewed beneath the skies.
In the quiet, truth takes flight,
In shadowed streets, we find our light.

Solitude Beneath the Umbrella

Beneath the canopy so wide,
Quiet moments, peace inside.
Raindrops dance on fabric bright,
Solace found in gentle light.

Worlds beyond, yet still we stay,
Wrapped in warmth, come what may.
Thoughts unspooled like threads of time,
In solitude, we find our rhyme.

Colors merge in soft embrace,
Life slows down, we find our place.
Drifting gently on the street,
With each heartbeat, life feels sweet.

Underneath this shelter's dome,
We are never far from home.
In stillness, visions come alive,
Solitude invites us to thrive.

Moments stretch and softly blend,
In the quiet, we transcend.
Beneath the stars, we shall dwell,
Finding peace and loving well.

Dance of the Droplets

Tiny beads on leaves sway,
In the breeze, they laugh and play.
Whispers of the morning light,
Nature's jewels, pure and bright.

They twirl down from clouds above,
Each drop a token, a sign of love.
Pattering softly on the ground,
A symphony of joy is found.

In puddles, they form little seas,
Reflecting life with graceful ease.
Watch them spin, a fleeting trance,
In this moment, droplets dance.

The earth awakens, colors burst,
In every droplet, wanderlust.
Each splash a tale of rain's embrace,
Bringing beauty to every place.

As day fades into amber shades,
The droplets twinkle, serenades.
In twilight's glow, their magic speaks,
In the silence, nature peaks.

When the Sky Weeps

The clouds gather with a sigh,
Heavy hearts in the vast sky.
A rumble echoes, thunder rolls,
Nature's tears, they cleanse our souls.

Raindrops fall like gentle tears,
Washing away all our fears.
Each droplet holds a whispered prayer,
In every storm, there's love to share.

The world glistens, fresh and new,
Each blade of grass, a brighter hue.
Waiting for the sun to peek,
In the silence, the earth will speak.

Moments pause, as the sky grieves,
In every sorrow, hope perceives.
A rainbow forms, bright and bold,
After the tears, its story told.

When the sky weeps, it brings forth life,
Ending the stillness, calming strife.
With every storm, a chance to grow,
In the heart of the rain, we glow.

Melodies in the Monsoon

Raindrops fall like sweet refrain,
A gentle dance, a soft refrain.
Rustling leaves in harmony,
Nature sings in jubilee.

Thunder claps, a bass so deep,
In the storm, the secrets keep.
Wind carries whispers, soft and clear,
Melodies for those who hear.

Each drop a note in the air,
Crafting tunes beyond compare.
Puddles ripple, a rhythmic sound,
In the monsoon, joy abounds.

The skies provide a grand concerto,
Nature orchestrates the show.
From lightning strokes to clouds' embrace,
In every note, a sacred space.

As the rain fades, peace appears,
Echoing in our hearts and cheers.
Melodies linger, soft and sweet,
In the monsoon, life feels complete.

Reflections in the Water

A mirror held by nature's hand,
Shows the world as planned and grand.
Ripples dance with each soft breeze,
Whispers flow between the trees.

Colors blend, a painter's dream,
In the water, shadows gleam.
Every wave a story told,
In reflections, life unfolds.

Fish swim by, the surface breaks,
Secrets hidden, the water takes.
Moments captured, time stands still,
In this pond, dreams fulfill.

Sunset hues bring warmth and glow,
Painting ripples in a flow.
A canvas stretched, so wide, so near,
In these waters, all is clear.

Each glance reveals a hidden truth,
Nature's wisdom, blessed with youth.
In reflections, we find our place,
A journey woven with grace.

Serenity in a Storm

Winds howl like wolves in the night,
Yet in my heart, there's a gentle light.
Rain falls like whispers, soft and clear,
A dance of nature, I hold dear.

Branches sway, the trees bend low,
Yet peace within begins to grow.
In chaos, I find a quiet space,
A stillness wrapped in nature's grace.

The thunder rumbles, a proud display,
While I watch from a safe array.
Clouds collide in a brilliant fight,
I breathe in deeply, savor the sight.

Nature's fury, a wild song,
In the storm's heart, I feel I belong.
The rain's rhythm, a soothing balm,
In this tempest, I'm wrapped in calm.

As lightning flashes, bright and bold,
I find my story quietly told.
In moments like this, I truly see,
Serenity blooms, wild and free.

Raindrop Reverie

Each raindrop sings a gentle tune,
Reflecting colors of sun and moon.
They dance on leaves, a fleeting spark,
Whispers of joy in the quiet park.

In puddles formed, reflections play,
A canvas where dreams drift away.
Rippling echoes of laughter soar,
Lost in the rhythm, wanting more.

The world grows still, wrapped in gray,
As hidden treasures come out to play.
Chase the droplets, feel the thrill,
My heart awakens, spirits fill.

Skies weep softly, a tender grace,
While I wander in this sacred space.
Raindrops kiss the earth below,
In their embrace, my worries flow.

With every splash, a story shared,
Nature's music, I feel prepared.
To find the magic in each fall,
Raindrop reverie enthralls us all.

Beneath Drenching Clouds

Beneath the clouds, a world awakes,
Where shadows dance and daylight breaks.
The air is fresh, a scent so rare,
A promise held in droplets' care.

With every step, the earth sighs deep,
In puddles wide, reflections leap.
A symphony of whispers rise,
Beneath the drenching, stormy skies.

The trees stand tall, in nature's choir,
Reaching limbs to the rain's desire.
The wind's embrace, both wild and true,
As storms break free, bringing the blue.

Lost in moments that time forgets,
In calming drops, I have no regrets.
A fleeting dance on muddy ground,
In every splash, new dreams are found.

An emerald world, washed anew,
Where every raindrop feels like dew.
Beneath these clouds, I breathe in deep,
Finding solace in nature's sweep.

Reflections in a Puddle

A puddle forms on a quiet street,
Mirroring skies, a transient feat.
Footsteps pause, in wonder they stare,
At the world upside down, a moment rare.

Clouds drift slowly, painted in grey,
Whispers of dreams that fade away.
With every ripple, a memory sways,
Gliding softly in sun-kissed rays.

Children run, splashing around,
Echoes of laughter, joy unbound.
In the water, their blessings grow,
Reflections shimmer, a playful show.

The sun breaks through with a radiant beam,
Awakening life from its gentle dream.
As colors blend in the light's embrace,
In puddles, I see each dear face.

Nature's mirror, a fleeting glance,
Where moments lived weave a dance.
Each reflection, a story to tell,
In a simple puddle, I find my well.

Muffled Lullabies of the Downpour

Raindrops whisper softly, as night descends,
In rhythm with the heart, where silence blends.
Each droplet carries dreams, so sweet and deep,
In the hush of storms, the world will sleep.

Clouds weave their stories, in shadows' embrace,
Nature's lullaby, a soothing grace.
With every patter, worries drift away,
Muffled serenades, in twilight's sway.

Windows frame the dance, of water's song,
Reminding us that we, too, belong.
In puddles, reflections shimmer like stars,
Guiding lost souls, healing their scars.

The night drapes its cloak, in shades of gray,
While the symphony plays, come what may.
In the cradle of rain, hope finds release,
As dreams float gently, unaware of cease.

Solitude in the Shower

Steam rises like whispers, a veil of calm,
In the water's embrace, I find my balm.
Each droplet a note in a melody pure,
Revealing the thoughts that my heart must endure.

Alone with my shadows, the past drips away,
As warm rivers flow, they begin to sway.
Wrapped in my solitude, I quietly muse,
On the weight of the world, and the warmth of the blues.

The mirror fogs up, reflecting the soul,
In the solitude's song, I start to feel whole.
With every splash, I wash memories old,
Finding strength in the silence, so gentle yet bold.

I dance with the streams, in rhythm I sway,
As echoes of laughter from yesterday play.
The solitude comforts, a sweet, sacred hour,
In the heart of the shower, I gather my power.

Cleansing Rhythm

The water cascades, a cleansing embrace,
Melodies rise in this sacred space.
Washing away the dust of the day,
In this fluid dance, worries drift away.

With each splash, I feel life ignite,
Every droplet shining, pure and bright.
A rhythm of freedom, freeing my mind,
In the song of the stream, serenity find.

The echoes of droplets create a tune,
A harmony wrapped in the afternoon.
The world outside fades, a distant refrain,
In the cleansing rhythm, I shed my pain.

I twist and I turn, under the flow,
The water's caress helps my spirit grow.
In the heartbeat of moments, life starts to gleam,
In this cleansing rhythm, I live and dream.

A Dance with the Elements

Under the sky's vast, welcoming dome,
I spin with the winds, no longer alone.
The elements call, a chorus divine,
In harmony woven, our souls intertwine.

Raindrops join in a gentle ballet,
While sunlight breaks forth, in bright disarray.
I twirl with the thunder, embrace the storm,
In this cosmic dance, I feel transformed.

Earth cradles my feet, grounding my flight,
Water's cool touch brings visions of light.
With fire in my spirit, I leap and I sway,
In the dance with the elements, I find my way.

Each movement a whisper, each breath a prayer,
In nature's vast theater, I shed every care.
The wind lifts me high, where dreams spin and glide,
In this dance of existence, I'm free to reside.

The Gentle Fall

Leaves drift softly from the tree,
Whispers of change in the breeze.
Colors dance in golden light,
Preparing for the winter's night.

A carpet thick of amber and gold,
Stories of summers quietly told.
Nature's art in every hue,
A gentle fall, a world anew.

The air grows crisp, the days grow short,
Harvest moon in the evening court.
Each step crunched beneath the feet,
In the silence, a rhythmic beat.

Once vibrant greens now fade away,
As daylight bows to ending day.
Trees stand tall, but their branches bare,
Embrace the chill, the winter's care.

Close your eyes and breathe it in,
A time for peace, the soul's soft spin.
In the gentle fall, we find our grace,
Nature's heartbeat, a warm embrace.

Beneath the Silver Veil

Moonlight drapes the world in white,
Casting shadows through the night.
Whispers linger on the air,
Secrets kept, a dreamer's lair.

Stars peer down with quiet eyes,
Reflecting dreams that softly rise.
The silver veil enfolds the land,
A tranquil hush, a gentle hand.

Silhouettes of trees stand tall,
Guardians of the nighttime's call.
Rustling leaves in the cool, calm air,
A serenade beyond compare.

Footsteps echo on the ground,
In this stillness, peace is found.
Beneath the silver veil we tread,
Where every heart can dream ahead.

Nature's magic weaves its thread,
A tapestry where fears are shed.
In the darkness, find the light,
Beneath the silver veil of night.

Echoes in the Puddle

Rain falls softly, tapping light,
Creating ripples, pure delight.
Small reflections dance and play,
Echoes of a passing day.

Mirrored skies in a shallow pond,
A world transformed, quiet and fond.
Each droplet sings a gentle tune,
The heart responds, as dreams commune.

Footsteps splash with joyous sound,
In simple moments, joy is found.
Fragments of life in a pool,
Nature's canvas, soft and cool.

Colors blend and currents swirl,
Whispers of a secret world.
In the puddle, stories weave,
Echoes tell what we believe.

When the storm has had its say,
And the sun returns to play.
We find our joy in every stride,
In echoes of the world outside.

Caress of the Cool Mist

Morning breaks with gentle grace,
The world wraps in a soft embrace.
Cool mist rises, breathes anew,
Whispers secrets, old yet true.

Hills roll softly in the light,
As dawn breaks into day from night.
Nature stretches, yawns and sighs,
Underneath the painted skies.

Each blade of grass, a jewel bright,
Sparkles with dew, a pure delight.
The caress of mist, so serene,
Enfolds the earth in shades of green.

Birdsong weaves through the still air,
A symphony both sweet and rare.
In the coolness, find your peace,
In every moment, worries cease.

Let the mist guide your way today,
A gentle touch, a soft ballet.
In the embrace of nature's kiss,
Find your solace, your pure bliss.

Dappled Shadows on the Ground

Leaves dance softly, paths unfold,
Sunlight weaves through stories told.
Nature's quilt in green and gold,
Mysteries of the earth behold.

Footsteps whisper, secrets shared,
Underneath a bough ensnared.
Colors shift, a life declared,
In this shade, hearts are prepared.

Cascades of shadow, fleeting grace,
Time stands still in this embrace.
A gentle touch, a quiet place,
Nature's art, a slow-paced race.

Shadows dance, they come alive,
In this moment, we thrive.
Beneath the trees, we dive,
In dappled light, we feel the drive.

Dreams awaken, hopes abound,
In this world where peace is found.
Underneath the structure sound,
Life's heartbeat, profound and round.

Embracing the Deluge

Raindrops fall like whispered prayers,
Nature's rhythm, unbroken layers.
Footprints washed, the earth repairs,
In storms, we shed our worldly cares.

Clouds collide, a rumbling song,
Together fierce, they dance along.
In the tempest, we belong,
From the chaos, we grow strong.

Drenched in life, we spin and sway,
The downpour shows us the way.
Each droplet sings, come what may,
In embrace, the heart's ballet.

Puddles form, a mirror bright,
Reflecting dreams, pure delight.
In the deluge, we find light,
Through every storm, our souls take flight.

Winds may howl, but we stand fast,
Weathered but united, steadfast.
In every drop, the die is cast,
Together, we have unsurpassed.

The Art of Stillness in the Splash

Water ripples, a moment's grace,
In silence, we find our place.
A gentle pause, time slows its pace,
Within this calm, love's warm embrace.

Beneath the surface, echoes hum,
Nature's heartbeat, soft yet drum.
In each splash, our fears succumb,
Holding close what's yet to come.

Waves of thought, they ebb and flow,
In stillness, wisdom starts to grow.
With every drop, a chance to know,
Life's quiet truths that softly show.

The art of peace in every splash,
Textures blend and colors clash.
In tranquil waters, dreams will dash,
Finding beauty in the brash.

Serenity calls, the mind takes flight,
In this dance, we feel the light.
Each shimmer, every quiet night,
Holds the magic that feels so right.

Whispers of the Storm

Thunder rumbles, shadows play,
Ancient tales in clouds convey.
Whispers brush against the day,
Nature speaks in a wild ballet.

In the twilight, light fades fast,
Moments captured, shadows cast.
The tempest moves, a spell is cast,
In this chaos, we find vast.

Lightning flashes, a painter's brush,
Breaching silence, in the rush.
Each bolt a spark, a heart's hush,
In storm's embrace, we feel the crush.

Voices of the wind, they soar,
Echoing cries from every shore.
Through every storm, we seek for more,
Understanding lies at its core.

In the heart of storm, we stand,
Grasping tightly, hand in hand.
With whispers soft, across the land,
Together, we learn to withstand.

Forgotten Stories in the Wet

Mist clings to stones, where shadows play,
Tales of the past softly drift away.
Echoes of laughter, whispers of woe,
Beneath the damp earth, memories grow.

Rain taps the roof, a rhythmic song,
Carrying secrets where dreams belong.
Footsteps are silent, yet voices remain,
In every droplet, joy mixes with pain.

Grasses are heavy with glistening dew,
Each blade a witness to moments anew.
The rivers remember, the oceans confess,
In the quiet of nature, we find our rest.

Through fog and through mist, the stories unfold,
Of lovers and legends, of brave hearts bold.
As twilight embraces the lingering light,
Forgotten stories take flight into night.

So listen closely to the patter of rain,
For in every whisper, there's loss and gain.
The wet earth reveals all the paths we tread,
In the solace of silence, the heart's gently led.

Splashes of Serenity

Gentle waves kiss the shore at dawn,
Painting the world with a tranquil yawn.
Colors blend softly in morning's embrace,
A canvas of calm in this sacred space.

The sunlight dances on water's face,
Ripples of joy in a timeless place.
Murmurs of nature in perfect tune,
Harmony echoes beneath the moon.

Footprints are fleeting, washed away,
Yet memories linger where children play.
Laughter rings out as splashes arise,
In moments so simple, wonder lies.

Breezes carry whispers from far away,
Swaying the branches in delicate sway.
In the heart of the earth, we find our ground,
In splashes of serenity, peace is found.

So take a deep breath; let the calm in,
Find solace in places where dreams begin.
With each gentle wave, let worries release,
Splash into life, drink deeply of peace.

Waters That Whisper

In the stillness, the waters call,
Whispers of wisdom, the rise and the fall.
Beneath the surface, secrets abide,
Tales of the ages that flow with the tide.

Moonlight reflects on a rippling brook,
Every wave tells the stories it took.
The rustle of leaves joins the song of the spray,
In harmony's embrace, night melds into day.

Ripples are messages from deep within,
Echoes of journeys of loss and of kin.
The calm waters hold every dream that we weave,
In their gentle embrace, we learn how to believe.

So lean by the shore and hear them speak,
The wisdom of waters, humble yet sleek.
In their soft murmurs, we gather the light,
Waters that whisper guide us through night.

In every droplet, in every sound,
Lies the promise of hope, in stillness profound.
Let the waters beckon, let their stories unfold,
In the dance of the currents, our hearts become bold.

Darkened Skies

Beneath darkened skies, shadows convene,
The air is thick with what might have been.
Raindrops like tears trace paths on the ground,
A world wrapped in silence, where sorrows abound.

Flashes of lightning, a moment of fire,
Illuminating thoughts that never tire.
Thunder rolls in, a distant lament,
Echoing fears that the heart has not spent.

Clouds gather closely, a blanket of gray,
Beating the drums of a storm on the way.
Yet in the chaos, there's beauty concealed,
In the heart of the tempest, the spirit is healed.

As darkness descends, the stars start to glow,
In the depths of the night, their light starts to show.
For even in shadows, there's hope to behold,
In darkened skies, brave stories unfold.

So dance in the rain, let the spirit ignite,
For after the storm, the future is bright.
Amidst all the turmoil, let love redefine,
In darkened skies, our hearts intertwine.

Brightened Souls

Through storms and through shadows, the light finds a way,
Brightened souls rise with the dawn of the day.
In the warmth of the sun, old wounds start to heal,
Each moment of kindness helps us to feel.

Colors awaken in the morning light,
Filling hearts with hope, banishing fright.
In laughter and joy, we gather as one,
Brightened souls dancing, our fears we outrun.

The echoes of love play a sweet melody,
Uniting our spirits in perfect harmony.
With hands intertwined, we tackle the chase,
Creating a world where all hearts find grace.

Through trials and triumphs, we learn and we grow,
With every shared moment, our spirits aglow.
In the tapestry woven, we're threads that entwine,
Brightened souls shining, our paths interline.

So let us rejoice in the journey ahead,
With passion and purpose, we'll carry the tread.
For together we rise, in this glorious role,
In a world full of wonders, we are brightened souls.